THE CHANGING FACE OF
IRELAND

Text by KAY BARNHAM
Photographs by CHRIS FAIRCLOUGH

HODDER
Wayland

an imprint of Hodder Children's Books

Produced for Hodder Wayland by
White-Thomson Publishing Ltd
2/3 St Andrew's Place
Lewes BN7 1UP

Editor: Stephen White-Thomson
Designer: Christopher Halls at Mind's Eye Design, Lewes
Additional picture research: Shelley Noronha, Glass Onion Pictures
Proofreader: Alison Cooper
Indexer: Patricia Baker

First published in Great Britain in 2003 by Hodder Wayland, an imprint of
Hodder Children's Books.

British Library Cataloguing in Publication Data
    Barnham, Kay
    The Changing Face of Ireland
    1. Ireland - Juvenile literature
    I. Title II. Ireland
    941.5'0824

ISBN 0 7502 4072 5

Printed in Hong Kong

Hodder Children's Books
A division of Hodder Headline Limited
338 Euston Road, London NW1 3BH

Acknowledgements
The publishers would like to thank
the following for their contributions
to this book: Rob Bowden – statistics
research; Peter Bull – map
illustration; Nick Hawken – statistics
panel illustrations. All photographs
are by Chris Fairclough except:
Camera Press 36; Corbis 24, 30; Eye
Ubiquitous 16, 29; Impact Photos 44;
Popperfoto 6, 7, 28, 34, 41. The
photo of Evelyn Cusack on page 11
is courtesy of RTÉ.

Contents

Cork: Past, Present and Future

Ireland is formed of four areas – Leinster, Munster, Connaught and Ulster – which are in turn divided into 32 counties. Of these, 26 counties form the Republic of Ireland and the remaining six counties form Northern Ireland. The Republic of Ireland is usually referred to as 'Ireland'. Its capital city is Dublin.

Cork is Ireland's second-biggest city and, ever since it was founded in the seventh century, it has played a major role in the country's eventful history. The city saw bloody fighting during Viking, Norman and English invasions; 2.5 million people emigrated from the nearby port of Cobh during and after the Famine of the 1840s; and violence erupted again during the Anglo-Irish and civil wars in the early twentieth century.

▲ *Cork has a mixture of older buildings and brand-new housing developments.*

Changes in Cork

Today, the many changes taking place throughout Ireland are reflected in Cork. Its population is growing every year, fuelled by a high birth rate, Irish citizens returning to their homeland, and newcomers of other nationalities.

There is also evidence of improvements to the country's transport network. During 2001, 1.8 million passengers used Cork International Airport – an increase of 5.7 per cent on the previous year. A new motorway currently under construction between Cork and Dublin will improve travel still further. Cork is meeting the challenge of modern life, while retaining its own unique, vibrant, friendly character.

▶ *The English Market in Cork is packed with fresh produce. It's also a good place to meet friends.*

Malin Head

North Channel

DONEGAL
Londonderry

Donegal

NORTHERN
IRELAND
Belfast

Ulster

Sligo

MAYO
SLIGO
LEITRIM
MONAGHAN
CAVAN
Dundalk

Connaught
ROSCOMMON
LONGFORD
LOUTH

IRISH
SEA

GALWAY
WEST
MEATH
MEATH
DUBLIN

N

ATLANTIC

OCEAN

Galway

REPUBLIC

OF

IRELAND

Dublin

OFFALY
KILDARE

LAOIS
WICKLOW
Wicklow

Leinster

0   75 km
0   50 miles

CLARE

Limerick

CARLOW

LIMERICK

TIPPERARY
Tipperary

Kilkenny

KILKENNY
WEXFORD

KERRY
Tralee

Munster

Waterford
Wexford

Dingle Bay
Killarney

CORK
WATERFORD

Carrantuohill
1041m
River Lee

St George's Channel

Bantry

Cork
Cobh

Celtic

Kinsale

Sea

▲ *This map shows the main geographical features of Ireland, as well as most places mentioned in this book.*

IRELAND: KEY FACTS

Area: 70,282 square km

Population: 3.84 million (mid-2001 estimate)

Population density: 54 people per square km

Capital city: Dublin (953,000)

Other main cities: Cork (180,000); Limerick (79,000); Galway (57,000); Waterford (44,000)

Highest mountain: Carrantuohill (1,041 m)

Longest river: Shannon (386 km)

Languages spoken: English, Irish

Main religions: Roman Catholic (91.5 per cent); Protestant (1.8 per cent); Presbyterian (3.75 per cent); Methodist (1.5 per cent)

Currency: Euro (1 euro = 100 cents)

2 Past Times

For hundreds of years, people have arrived on Ireland's shores eager to settle or even to rule the island. From the seventeenth until the early twentieth century the country was a British colony. After countless rebellions by the Irish people, negotiations were held between the two countries. The British proposed that Ireland should be divided into two parts – Partition. They said that the Irish should rule themselves, except in the northern six counties, where many people were loyal to Great Britain. This area should remain under British rule. Not everyone in Ireland agreed with this proposal. In a bloody civil war, they fought over whether to accept the offer of Irish rule for most of the country, or to rebel until it was granted to all 32 counties.

The Irish Free State

Those who agreed with Partition gained the upper hand and, in 1921, the Irish Free State was born. In 1949 it became the Republic of Ireland, with its own constitution. But the underlying disagreements about British rule were never really solved, as the continuing troubles in Northern Ireland show. However, the 1998 Good Friday Agreement began a peace process that will hopefully bring an end to unrest in Northern Ireland.

▲ The Celtic cross is a symbol that dates back to the Celts, early inhabitants of Ireland.

▼ British Prime Minister Tony Blair and Irish Taoiseach Bertie Ahern sign the Good Friday Agreement in April 1998.

The EEC and EU

In 1973 Ireland joined the EEC (now the European Union or EU). As a member of the EU, Ireland has benefited enormously from financial aid and improved trade with Europe. There have also been drawbacks to membership, though, with some restrictions on fishing and farm production.

▼ *Bertie Ahern supported the 'Yes' vote in the Nice Treaty referendum. Irish people were asked to decide whether or not to agree to the enlargement of the EU.*

IN THEIR OWN WORDS

'My name is Noreen Collins and I'm proud to be Irish. When I travel overseas, I like to wear something white, gold and green, to show where I'm from. Ireland has changed since I was young. For the last four generations, our land was used for farming, but now there's no money in it for small farms. People used to be self-sufficient and now they just eat fast food. It's as if supermarkets are taking over our lives. And there were no new houses built around here for over a hundred years – now they're springing up like daffodils all over the country.'

Landscape and Climate

Ireland is the most north-westerly country in Europe. It is bordered by Northern Ireland and separated from Scotland, England and Wales by the Irish Sea.

Coasts

Ireland's coast is 3,172 km in length and varies considerably from county to county. Whereas the east and south-east coasts sweep gently into the sea, the west and south-west coasts feature rugged peninsulas, sheer cliffs and wide beaches, with remote islands scattered offshore.

The west coast has seen many historic moments. In 1588 ships from the Spanish Armada were wrecked here. In 1856, a transatlantic cable was laid from County Kerry to Newfoundland, Canada; two years later, the cable was used to transmit the first transatlantic telegram, from Queen Victoria to President Buchanan in the US.

▲ *Ireland has many beautiful beaches with crystal-clear water.*

Hills and mountains

Compared to other parts of Europe, Ireland's hills and mountains are relatively small – the highest, Carrantuohill, is just over a thousand metres. They are located mainly around the edges of the island, with the higher mountain ranges in the west. Washed clean by the weather, the bare limestone hills of the Burren region are low, but dramatic.

▼ *Most of the mountain ranges are found near Ireland's coasts. Trees have been planted along their slopes, and in the valleys.*

Lowlands

The central part of the country is low-lying and wet. Most of the country's lakes, or loughs, are here, as are most of the bogs and marshes. Bogs are areas of wetland with acid, peaty soil.

▼ *The lowlands in central Ireland are where much of the country's peat is found.*

IN THEIR OWN WORDS

'My name is Donal Kearney and I've worked as a forester for 25 years. Forests are found in all parts of Ireland, usually on land that isn't good enough for crops. During that time I've seen lots of changes in the business – we used to use horses to cart away the timber, but now modern machinery makes the whole job much easier. The weather is wetter than it used to be, but it doesn't really affect forestry. Sitting on my machine, high up a mountainside on a bright spring day, watching the lambs and the wildlife, makes this the best job in the world!'

The Emerald Isle

The Gulf Stream and south-westerly winds that blow from the Atlantic control the weather. Ireland does not suffer from extremes of temperature – it does not usually rise much above 20 °C or fall far below freezing.

Named the Emerald Isle because of its vivid green landscape, Ireland can be a very wet place to live. The most rain falls in the north-west, west and south-west of the country, especially over higher ground. In 2000, for example, 1,786 mm of rain fell in Kerry in the west, compared to 840 mm in Dublin, on the east coast.

However, it does not rain all the time – south-westerly winds mean that the weather can be very changeable; it is not uncommon to experience several sunny spells and rain showers in one day. The south-east is the sunniest place in Ireland. In 2000, Wexford enjoyed an average of 4.7 hours of sunshine a day, compared to just 3.7 in Kerry.

▲ On rainy days, the mountain tops are often hidden by cloud.

◄ Ireland rarely suffers from very heavy rain, but it is often drizzly.

IN THEIR OWN WORDS

'My name is Evelyn Cusack and I'm a meteorologist for RTÉ – one of Ireland's television channels. Ireland is the first port of call for many of the weather systems that move across the North Atlantic. We rarely get torrential downpours and thunderstorms, but we do get a lot of 'soft days', when the weather is mild and misty with light drizzle. During the last few winters, we've had very little frost, and the weather has become cloudier. However, it's difficult to say whether these weather conditions are part of natural climate variability or a result of global warming.'

Climate change

Since the beginning of the twentieth century, Ireland's climate has become gradually warmer. Data recorded at Malin Head in County Donegal show that between 1910 and 2000 the temperature rose by around 1 °C. Rainfall figures seem to show that the climate is getting wetter, but it remains to be seen how this will affect an island that is famous for its rain.

▼ *Despite its reputation for rain, Ireland can be a very sunny place too!*

4 Natural Resources

Fossil fuels (including coal, gas and peat) provide 94 per cent of Ireland's electricity. However, the Irish government aims to reduce dependency on coal and peat, increase the use of oil and double the use of natural gas and renewable energy by 2010.

Renewable energy

Ireland is one of the leading producers of wind energy in Europe, especially along the west coast of the country. It is hoped that this and other forms of renewable energy, such as wave power and hydroelectric power, will become more common in the future.

Bogs

Peat bogs form in very wet places and are made up of layer upon layer of the partly rotted remains of dead trees and plants. Over a sixth of the total area of Ireland is bogland. Large quantities of peat are dug for domestic and industrial fuel and it provides about 10 per cent of Ireland's electricity, but action is being taken to ensure that peat is conserved in the future. This is because boglands are home to many rare and protected species of plants and animals. They are also an important part of Ireland's history and scenery.

▲ These blocks of peat have been laid out to dry.

▼ Many of Ireland's peat bogs are now protected, to prevent damage being done to areas of natural beauty.

IN THEIR OWN WORDS

'My name's David Lewis and I work in a quarry in Kilkenny. The quarry employs 70 staff altogether. We quarry limestone, which is used for a great variety of things – buildings, gravestones and monuments. Our stone is also used for streetscape work – paving, kerbing and guttering. We sell within Ireland, but also export a lot of stone to Belgium, the Netherlands, Germany and the USA. Within Europe, it helps to use the euro because we know what we're working with – there aren't any currency fluctuations to worry about, so the price of our product doesn't change from day to day.'

Minerals

Discoveries of new mineral deposits in the last century have boosted the country's mining industry. In 1999, mineral output included 223,000 tonnes of zinc (the biggest deposit is at Navan, County Meath) and 39,000 tonnes of lead. Ireland is one of the leading exporters of these minerals in Europe. Slate, limestone, sandstone and quartzite are also quarried.

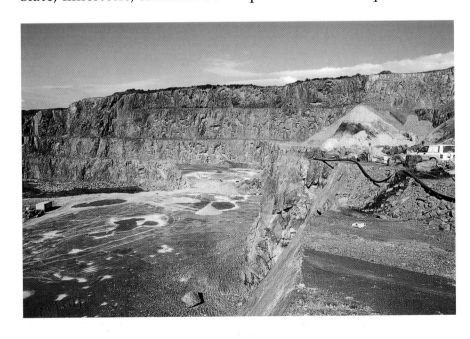

◀ *Explosives are used to blast away material and quarry deep into the ground.*

Agriculture

About a fifth of Ireland is arable land and much of the rest is used for pasture. The best farmland is in the east and south-east, where the weather is less harsh. Raising animals earns farmers the most money, followed by poultry production. The main crops are wheat, barley, oats, sugar beet and potatoes.

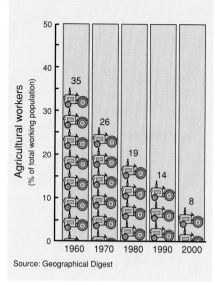

▲ *The number of Irish agricultural workers has fallen dramatically since 1960.*

◀ *Livestock is one of the most profitable type of farming.*

When the Irish Free State was formed Ireland was cut off from the industry around Belfast (which is in the region that remains under British rule), so agriculture was by far the most important and successful contributor to the country's economy. Most of the farms were, and still are, small and family-run.

▼ *On a small, family farm, the farmer cannot usually afford to run much machinery.*

The European Union

When Ireland joined the EEC (now the EU) European prices for produce were controlled. This meant that farmers received a good price for their meat and dairy products, as the EEC promised to buy leftover goods to ensure that prices stayed high. (If there is too much of one product on the market, prices come down.)

◄ *It takes more machinery to look after a bigger farm.*

This system has now been changed. Rather than producing goods that will not sell, the EU is encouraging farmers to rear or grow more profitable products. Farmers may now have to choose to grow other crops, or may decide to sell their land to owners of bigger farms, who have the machinery to run a farm more cheaply and so make more money.

IN THEIR OWN WORDS

'My name is Paddy Murphy and I'm a strawberry farmer in Wexford. This used to be a dairy farm, but now strawberries are more profitable. I grow strawberries in plastic tunnels so that I have more control over the amount of warmth and water they get, and I don't use herbicides or insecticides. All of my produce is sold within Ireland, most of it to large supermarkets. I employ workers from overseas during the busy months of the year, but I can manage this place on my own most of the time, as almost all of the watering and fertilizing is done automatically.'

5

The Changing Environment

About 35 per cent of the country's population lives in Dublin, with another 7 per cent living in Cork. Over half of all people live less than 10 km from the coast, which puts burdens on the roads and public services of those areas.

Housing

The population of Ireland's cities is rising. Although old cottages are common in rural areas, the majority of housing is much newer. The number of new houses built more than doubled between 1992 and 2000 to 49,812. Developers are now being urged to make more use of derelict urban areas, rather than building on more of the country's green-belt areas.

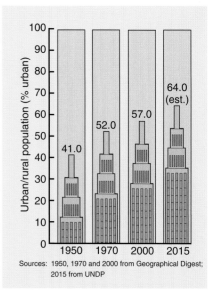

Sources: 1950, 1970 and 2000 from Geographical Digest; 2015 from UNDP

▼ *A few houses are still being built in green-belt areas, but this is becoming less common.*

▲ *It is estimated that almost two-thirds of Irish people will live in towns and cities by 2015.*

Rural environmental issues

Ireland is a place where trees grow easily and it is estimated that, centuries ago, two-thirds of the country was covered in forests, which decayed to become today's bogs. But by 1900 thousands of trees had been felled to make way for fields. At this time, a mere 1 per cent of the country was still forested. Drastic action was needed and a programme to reintroduce forests was begun. In 1999, tree-cover had risen to 9 per cent and the figure is still rising. The Irish government is committed to increasing the area covered by forests in order to promote the environment, tourism and forest-based industry.

▲ *Forestry is becoming a more important industry, and new trees are being planted all the time. Logging is carefully controlled.*

IN THEIR OWN WORDS

'My name is Andrew Woodward and I'm project-managing the construction of a new section of motorway between Cork and Dublin. In general, the roads in Ireland aren't that bad, although some do need maintenance. Our job is part of a strategic plan by the Irish government to improve communication routes between major cities. We have to comply with EU rules about keeping pollution to a minimum and, before work began, archaeologists came on site to search for evidence of historical settlements. We haven't faced much opposition, as local people see the new road as being of benefit to the community and to Ireland.'

The environment

Ireland's population is expected to rise to over 4 million by 2011, increasing pressure on the country's resources and the environment. The country's main challenges are to improve the treatment of waste water, reduce solid waste and cut greenhouse-gas emissions.

Air pollution

It is hoped that the problem of greenhouse-gas emissions can be reduced by using natural gas, rather than coal or peat, to run power stations. If Ireland reaches its proposed target of increasing tree-cover from 9 per cent to 17 per cent of the country, then this will also help to tackle the problem. Trees absorb carbon dioxide, which is a major greenhouse gas.

At the end of the last century, action was taken to deal with the problem of air pollution caused by smoky coal. Smokeless zones were introduced in heavily populated areas, where the sale and use of bituminous fuel was banned. The scheme was considered a success and the smokeless zones are still being extended.

▶ *Peat briquettes produce far less smoke than some types of coal.*

IN THEIR OWN WORDS

'My name is Naomi Daly and I'm from Kerry. Nearly 4 million people live in Ireland so a lot of rubbish is generated. Some things help to improve this situation: these bags for life can be recycled. A big issue in the news at the moment is whether it's better to incinerate rubbish or to dump it. Smog is a problem in big cities like Dublin and Cork, but it's improving, and the air is cleaner in the countryside. The government should be stricter with big companies who pollute – they don't get fined enough right now.'

Water pollution

Agricultural pollution, especially phosphorous output, is one of the main contributors to water pollution in Ireland – it can cause great harm to wildlife and the environment. Stricter environmental controls have been introduced to cut this risk. Meanwhile, new schemes are improving waste-water treatment. In 2003, Cork's brand-new sewer network and water treatment works were completed to deal effectively with the 60 million litres of raw sewage and polluted water that once flowed into the River Lee every day.

▼ *Water treatment works are improving the quality of Ireland's water.*

Recycling

Recycling is on the increase in Ireland, but it has a long way to go before it reaches the standard of other European countries. Most Irish people are eager to improve their environment – the main problem seems to be that they do not yet have enough information about the ways that this can be achieved, or the right facilities.

Dealing with waste

The Irish government is considering many different ways of reducing waste and increasing recycling. An important step will be to boost the numbers of 'bring sites', where people bring glass and other materials to be recycled. Austria, for example, currently has 13 times as many 'bring sites' per head of population as Ireland – 2.8 sites per thousand people.

▼ *This man is helping the environment by recycling his newspapers.*

As far as glass is concerned, it has been suggested that Ireland follow Denmark's lead. Denmark reuses a colossal 450,000 tonnes of glass waste every year. Danes are encouraged to return glass bottles after use, so that they can be refilled and used again. This cuts down on the number of plastic bottles used and promotes reuse, which is much better for the environment than recycling.

Bags for life

In 2002, the Irish government made a positive step towards reducing plastic waste. They introduced an environment tax on all plastic carrier bags and encouraged shoppers to buy and reuse hard-wearing shopping bags instead – these are later recycled. The scheme has been very successful.

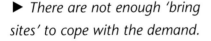

▶ *There are not enough 'bring sites' to cope with the demand.*

IN THEIR OWN WORDS

'My name is Flor McCarthy and I live in Kinsale. My wife and I have four children, so our family produces a lot of rubbish! We've been recycling for eight years, but it's not been easy, as there are only three recycling facilities in Cork, although we've been promised another fifteen. (Most waste still goes to landfill sites. A lot of rubbish is incinerated, but many people are against this, as it pollutes the air.) As well as recycling bottles, card, paper and plastics, we also recycle building materials. Our house is built with lots of second-hand bricks, timber and doors.'

6

The Changing Population

When compared with the United Kingdom, Ireland is very sparsely populated. In the UK, an average of 244 people live in each square kilometre, while only 54 people live in the same area in Ireland. However, per square kilometre, Ireland is home to almost twice as many people as the USA!

A youthful country

Census information shows that the population of Ireland is getting older (the average age in 1996 was 33.6, compared with 30.8 in 1981) and that fewer children are being born. However, the country still has the highest birth rate and the youngest population in Europe.

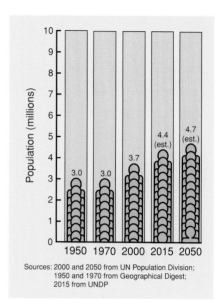

Sources: 2000 and 2050 from UN Population Division; 1950 and 1970 from Geographical Digest; 2015 from UNDP

▲ The Irish population is predicted to continue growing steadily.

◄ Over 40 per cent of the Irish population is under the age of 25.

Life expectancy

In 1926, the average life expectancy was 57.4 years for men and 57.9 years for women. By 1996, this had risen to 73 years for men. Women can expect to live until they are 78.7 years old. These massive increases are linked to improved diet and healthcare. However, smoking is still a cause for concern. It is estimated that a third of the Irish population smokes, causing a fifth of all deaths every year.

The Irish health service provides free healthcare for people on low incomes and for their families. Financial assistance is available for other people, depending on how much they earn. Alternative medicine, such as homeopathy, aromatherapy and acupuncture, is now becoming more widely available.

◀ *Life expectancy increased dramatically during the twentieth century but women still live longer than men.*

IN THEIR OWN WORDS

'My name is Mairead Hartnett and I live in Dublin. My mother married late, at 32, but my gran was married at 17. I would like to get married, but need to meet the right guy first! Then I'd like to have four children – although people seem to be having fewer children, many Irish families are still quite large. As regards marriage, the general attitude now is that people live together for a while first. Also, there's a new freedom to travel. People used to marry partners within cycling distance, now we've got the whole world!'

The Famine and emigration

In 1845, 8.5 million people lived in Ireland. At this time, the population was highly dependent on the potato, which was cheap to produce and provided a healthy diet. They sold their more valuable crops to survive. When a disease called potato blight attacked in 1845, many of the potato crops failed. During the next three years, they failed again and again. By 1851, a million people had died from hunger and disease and a million more had emigrated.

After the Famine, millions more Irish people went abroad in search of work, using their earnings to support the families they left behind. The population continued to dwindle. For most of the last century, under 3 million people lived in Ireland, with many young people emigrating when they were old enough to do so.

◀ *A statue in Cobh commemorating the large number of Irish people who emigrated in the mid-nineteenth century.*

Immigration

However, the population has been rising steadily since the 1970s. Employment and economic prospects have improved, luring back Irish people and encouraging those of other nationalities to live there. In 1996, 7 per cent of those living

IN THEIR OWN WORDS

'My name is Catherine Buchanan and I'm from Vancouver, Canada. I've been living in Ireland for eighteen months – I moved here with my husband, who is a civil engineer working for a construction company. I work in a solicitor's office now, but I found it difficult to get a job to begin with as it took ten weeks for my work permit to be approved. This put a lot of potential employers off. Ireland is a fantastic place to live – the pace of life is very relaxed and everyone is very friendly. However, I do miss the hustle and bustle of Vancouver!'

in Ireland were born elsewhere – almost half were from the UK. Four hundred thousand Irish citizens now living in Ireland have lived abroad at some time. The UK is the most popular destination.

But for many there is no place like home. In 1996, three-quarters of Irish people still lived in the county in which they were born.

▶ *A bustling street scene in Dublin. As work prospects have improved, thousands of Irish people have moved back to Ireland to live and work.*

7

Changes at Home

Irish families have changed considerably since the nineteenth century. After the Famine (1845–1849), people only usually got married if they could afford to support a family. The 1926 census shows that 84 per cent of male farm labourers aged 45–54 had never married, compared to only 21 per cent of farmers.

◄ Today, many women are choosing to have fewer children.

▼ Men are now more involved with childcare.

Religious beliefs meant that birth control was frowned upon, and in 1911 the average completed family included 6.5 children. However, this had little effect on the size of the country's population because emigration figures were also high. By 1981, when marriage had become as popular as it was before the Famine, more relaxed attitudes to birth control meant that the average number of children per family was 2.2. In 1996, the figure was just 1.18 children.

Family structure

The traditional family structure is changing too. The number of single-parent families has grown and co-habiting couples make up almost 4 per cent of family units. Although divorce only became legal in 1995, the number of broken marriages more than doubled between 1986 and 1996.

Irish women are having children later in life, or not having children at all. The average age of all mothers in 1980 was 28.8 years, rising to 30.2 years in 2000. In 1996, 28 per cent of all couples in the 25–34 age group had no children, compared with 16 per cent in 1986.

▶ *The average age of women having their first child rose by 1.4 years between 1980 and 2000.*

IN THEIR OWN WORDS

'My name is Kay O'Brien and I'm from Clare. Lots of things have changed in Ireland during my lifetime. Thirty years ago, the Irish were all trying to leave the country – my eldest son emigrated to Australia. Now, the Aussies are coming to live here! I'm happy with my life – it's easier than my mother's. In fact, nowadays, life is easier for most women. We don't have to get up early and go to the bog to dig the turf, as my mother used to do. As for my daughters, I don't mind where they live, or with whom, just as long as they're happy.'

The Roman Catholic Church

On the whole, the Irish population is religious and overwhelmingly Roman Catholic (91.5 per cent). The size of congregations has fallen, but many people do still attend church once a week, especially in rural areas. Over twenty other denominations make up the remaining 8.5 per cent of the population, and of these, members of the Church of Ireland, Protestants, Presbyterians, Methodists, Muslims and Jehovah's Witnesses are the largest groups.

Pilgrimages

The most devout Roman Catholics show their faith by taking part in religious pilgrimages. These include an annual pilgrimage to the summit of Croagh Patrick – a holy mountain in County Mayo, where it is said that Saint Patrick once fasted for 40 days. Many people make the 765-metre climb in bare feet.

Each year, thousands of Roman Catholics visit a small holy island in the centre of Lough Derg – a lake in County Donegal. Pilgrims show their faith by taking part in an extremely tough pilgrimage, which involves spending three days fasting, walking and praying – all barefoot.

▲ Simple Roman Catholic shrines are dotted around the countryside. Like this one, most are dedicated to the Virgin Mary.

◀ A bare-footed pilgrim climbs up Croagh Patrick, one of 25,000 people who make the pilgrimage every July.

IN THEIR OWN WORDS

'My name is Jonathan Buckley and I live in Kinsale. I'm Roman Catholic and I go to Mass every Sunday. When I'm older, I think I'll still go. More people go to church in the country than in towns. There's a very tense atmosphere in church – I'd prefer it if services were conducted in a more relaxed way, with up-to-date music and singing. Also, there should be more women preachers and priests. I think male priests lead too secluded a life to know much about real life. Although we study religion at school, my friends and I never discuss religion outside the classroom.'

The patron saint of Ireland

St Patrick's Day is celebrated on 17 March. Many people enjoy watching or taking part in bright, colourful and musical parades held in towns and cities around Ireland. St Patrick's Day is also celebrated all around the world – in places as far afield as New York, USA, and Sydney, Australia – by the descendants of the millions who emigrated from Ireland in the past. Celebrations outside the country are often more extravagant than those actually in Ireland.

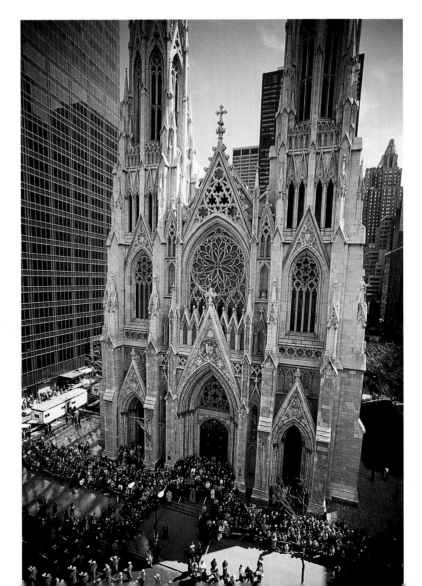

▶ *The annual St Patrick's Day Parade passes St Patrick's Cathedral in New York.*

Education

Irish students are staying in education longer and leaving with more qualifications. The number of students aged 15 and over increased by 20 per cent between 1991 and 1996; the percentage of people aged 20–24 in further and higher education rose by 6 per cent. These increases may have been influenced by the fact that college and university education recently became free.

The Irish school system is based around two main sets of exams. The Junior Cert is taken by students aged 14–15 years and covers Irish, Maths, English, History, Geography, Religion, either French or German, and other subjects of the student's choice. Leaving Cert exams are taken at the age of 18–19 years. Irish and English are compulsory, but the students can choose their other subjects, although they must pass a total of six subjects.

▲ *A school in Ireland welcomes one of the country's most famous citizens, Mary Robinson, a former president of Ireland, to their morning assembly.*

The Irish language

Ireland has two official languages – Irish and English. Official documents, such as birth certificates and driving licences, are printed in Irish and English, and the names of many major public organizations are in Irish. For example, the post office is called Oifig an Phoist.

The Dingle Peninsula in County Kerry is one of the last places in Ireland where people spoke Irish as a first language. These areas are known as Gaeltacht. The spoken language is still very much in evidence here.

▶ *In Ireland, most road signs feature both Irish and English place names.*

IN THEIR OWN WORDS

'My name is Margaret Kelleher and I'm a teacher in an all-boys' Roman Catholic state school in Cork city. The girls' school is next door. Lots of city schools teach boys and girls separately, although in the countryside schools are usually mixed. I teach all subjects. A lack of resources causes problems, as do changes to the curriculum – we need more time to retrain. In the new curriculum, pupils only learn to speak Irish – they don't have to learn how to write it. This seems to be because the Irish language has no place in business in Ireland today.'

Irish food

When potatoes arrived in Ireland in the eighteenth century, they were an expensive food enjoyed by the rich. They only became popular in the following century, when people realized how cheap and easy it was to live on them. But when the potato blight struck, so did the Famine (see page 24), showing that the country couldn't rely on one type of food. However, potatoes such as Kerr's Pinks and Golden Wonder are still an important part of the Irish diet.

Many traditional Irish foods date back to before the introduction of the potato. Top Irish chefs have revived interest in these foods and cook meals using many famous Irish ingredients. These include black pudding, carrageen moss and many types of cheese, such as Gubbeen.

The famous Oyster Festival held in Galway every September celebrates another of Ireland's traditional foods. Locally farmed oysters are swallowed in their thousands, washed down with Ireland's most famous export – Guinness.

▼ Soda bread is a traditional type of bread that is made with buttermilk.

Healthy living

As elsewhere, supermarkets and fast-food outlets have made new foods available to Ireland. Dietitians worry that the population eats too much meat and dairy produce and not enough fruit and pulses. The Irish have a reputation for heavy drinking, but this is not supported by recent evidence. Many Irish people are teetotal – they don't drink at all.

◀ *Irish people are being encouraged to eat more fruit and vegetables to improve their health.*

IN THEIR OWN WORDS

'My name is Carmel Buckley and I'm Assistant Director of Public Health for Nursing. I like to cook traditional Irish meals – I learnt the recipes from my mother. My family and I keep fit – we walk or swim most days. I work as a nurse and midwife, and I advise mothers to breastfeed if possible and then to use fresh produce. Smoking is a huge problem amongst teenage girls. They seem to be more interested in keeping thin than worrying about their future health. I think the fashion industry is to blame – all the models seem to smoke.'

Leisure time

Irish people are very family-orientated and sociable. The pub is often the social centre of a community; children are welcome and it's frequently the venue for traditional music and singing. Special occasions such as weddings would not be complete without several guests making a musical contribution.

Popular sports

In 1884, the Gaelic Athletic Association (GAA) successfully reintroduced many traditional Irish sports to the country, including Gaelic football, hurling and camogie. These and many other sports are very popular, both with those who like to play and with those who like to watch.

▼ *Hurling is popular with players of all ages.*

Gaelic football is a mixture of rugby and American football. The game is exciting and action-packed. It is interesting to note that more women play and watch Gaelic football in Ireland than play and watch football in the UK.

Hurling is similar to hockey, but is played with raised sticks. It is fast, furious and requires great skill. Hurling is becoming increasingly popular – in 2002, 84,000 people attended one match. Camogie is a gentler version of the sport for women.

Football has become increasingly popular since Ireland first reached the World Cup Finals in 1990, and competed again in 1994 and 2002. Rugby is another favourite sport and basketball too is gaining in popularity.

▼ *Ireland's football supporters are very loyal. Here they are celebrating their 1-1 draw with Germany in the 2002 World Cup.*

IN THEIR OWN WORDS

'My name is Lorna O'Brien and I live in Donegal. Irish sports are very popular in this country. Gaelic football is played in most schools. Hurling and camogie are only played in Ireland, so counties play each other. I think it's best these sports are only played here. As for me, sport is very important. I try to keep fit and eat healthily so that I perform well on the running track. Last year, I competed in the All Ireland Championships – I came fourth in the 200 metres! But it's the friends I've made through sport that make it so special for me.'

Road bowling is a traditional sport now limited to one or two parts of Ireland. Crowds of people follow each game, the object being to throw the heavy ball as far as possible down a twisty country lane.

▼ *With so many kilometres of coastline, there is plenty of room for sailing and other watersports.*

8 Changes at Work

Ireland suffered from high unemployment for much of the twentieth century. The main reason for this was that while it was a British colony Ireland's economy was linked with that of Britain. After Partition, in 1921, Britain's support was removed and Ireland had to develop its own economy. This resulted in high levels of unemployment, which peaked in the 1930s and in the 1980s, when almost a fifth of men were out of work. For many people, emigration was the only way to escape unemployment.

The beginning of the twenty-first century has seen both unemployment and emigration fall. Between 2000 and 2002, unemployment was around 4 per cent – one of the lowest figures ever.

◄ The opening of new computer software premises – like this Microsoft office in Dublin – led to new work opportunities in the 1990s.

Fishing

Ireland may be a small country, but it has access to a large area of sea – 13 per cent of the EU's marine territory. Much of the catch is exported – of 325,000 tonnes of fish landed in 1997, almost four-fifths was sold to other countries. Just two years later, the catch had increased to 361,000. Shellfish – such as lobsters, crayfish and prawns – are the country's next biggest fish export.

Environmental concerns led to the Irish government banning drift-net fishing in 2002, to help prevent dolphins and other protected species from being caught in fishing nets. It remains to be seen what effect this will have on the Irish fishing industry.

▼ *The Irish fishing industry, underdeveloped in the past, is now booming.*

IN THEIR OWN WORDS

'My name is Paul O'Connell and I'm a fishmonger in the English Market in Cork city. Every morning, first thing, we take two vans to Castletownbere in West Cork and buy around 50 boxes of fish. Most of our fish – sole, mackerel, plaice, whiting, haddock and cod – is caught off the Irish coast, but other types – shark, swordfish, tuna, brill and turbot – are flown in daily from Europe, South America and the USA. Ireland also exports fish to countries such as Spain, France and Italy. One thing's for sure, there's plenty of fish in the sea around Ireland!'

'Irish' industry

It is estimated that at least a third of Irish industry is actually owned by foreign businesses. Many overseas companies choose to have their headquarters or major bases in Ireland, partly because the government offers tax benefits to companies that employ Irish workers. These industries are many and varied – from manufacturers and pharmaceutical companies to technical support services.

Ireland is now the second-largest exporter of software in the world – after the USA. Many software companies have based their businesses in Ireland because of the tax benefits and also the availability of an educated population to provide the necessary workforce.

The arrival of foreign companies has brought business to Ireland and has helped to reduce unemployment levels, but there is a downside. There is a danger that profits made by these companies will leave the country, rather than being

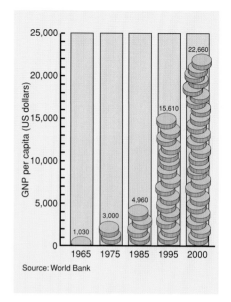

▲ Recently, GNP per capita has risen dramatically.

▼ This ferry is carrying export goods overseas.

reinvested in Ireland. Also, if foreign companies go through hard times and have to reduce the size of their workforce, they may decide to close down their offices or factories in Ireland. But, for the foreseeable future, everything is going well.

▼ *Irish companies provide technical support for computer users in many other countries.*

IN THEIR OWN WORDS

'My name is Brendan Kellet and I'm a training manager in a pharmaceutical company in Cork that's owned by a foreign company. I went to the University of Cork, then studied for an MA in England. I live about an hour's drive from work, but I leave early to avoid the traffic – it's worth travelling so that I can live in the country. It's a much better place to bring up children. My wife works different hours, so we employ a child minder and, as public transport is limited, we have two cars, so that we can both drive to work. I'd love to work four days a week, but it's unlikely it'll happen!'

Women in the workplace

The number of women employed outside the home has increased considerably since the 1970s. In 1971, only 28 per cent of women were employed, but by 1996, this had risen to 41 per cent.

   More women are returning to work after having children and there are many reasons for this. There are now laws that aim to ensure men and women are treated equally at work, maternity-leave conditions have improved and the cost of raising a family has risen. Since April 2000 a childcare programme funded by the Irish government and the EU has invested millions of euros in childcare services, making it easier for more women to return to work.

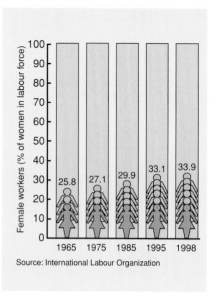

Source: International Labour Organization

▲ *The number of women in employment has risen steadily since 1965.*

◀ *Many more women can now take advantage of the independence that having their own income brings.*

The creative industry

Ireland has a rich history of creative talent, from famous authors such as James Joyce and Roddy Doyle to pop bands including The Corrs and U2. Poets, artists, folk bands and sculptors have all flourished here. The Irish government is so committed to ensuring that Ireland remains a popular place for artists of all kinds to live and work that they exempt certain groups of people from paying tax. This encourages artists to move to Ireland and gives others a very good reason to stay.

◀ *The Irish rock group U2 after winning five Grammy Awards in Los Angeles, USA, in 2002.*

IN THEIR OWN WORDS

'My name is Pattigail O'Connell. I'm a florist and I started my own business in 1993. I now employ two people part-time and firmly believe that if you treat your staff well, you are repaid with plenty of hard work. I rely on my computer to receive orders from all over the world and use it to search the Internet for information on suppliers and flowers. It isn't easy juggling work and home life, but I'm really lucky – my mother looks after my little boy two days a week. The housework does tend to suffer though!'

Tourism

More people visit Ireland than live there – in 2000, it is estimated that 6.7 million tourists visited the country. There are numerous reasons why Ireland is a popular holiday destination. Tourists come to experience the Irish way of life, the beautiful and varied scenery, the golf and fishing, and the many ancient archaeological sites. Descendants of the emigrants who left Ireland in the past often come to find out about their family's history. But, for whatever reason tourists visit, they mean big business for Ireland.

The large number of visitors in tourist 'hot spots' can put a strain on local roads and services, and can lead to environmental damage. With the number of tourists set to rise, the industry is trying to tackle this problem by promoting different areas of Ireland as tourist destinations.

▲ Tourists travel from all over the world to experience the Irish way of life.

◀ A tour guide tells a party of tourists all about the local sights.

Horse-racing

This has been popular in Ireland for many centuries. Thoroughbreds are bred here, horses are trained here and people enjoy going to the races here. There are estimated to be about 55,000 horses in Ireland – part of an industry that is worth millions of euros.

During 2001, both tourism and horse-racing were hit by the threat of foot and mouth disease. Millions of livestock had to be slaughtered in the UK, but the disease never made it to Ireland, thanks to tough rules enforced by the Irish government. And although the country lost money, this was nothing in comparison to the effect on agriculture if the disease had taken hold.

▼ *This racehorse is being shown at an agricultural show.*

IN THEIR OWN WORDS

'My name is Teddy McNamara. I work as a tourist guide, a builder and all-round entrepreneur! One of my favourite jobs is taking tourists round the town to show them the sights. Ireland is very popular with Americans – we're respected in the USA and they like to visit our country. Tourists come here from all over the world, which is great. I'm proud to be Irish, but I think that youngsters now regard themselves as being European instead. This is good for the community – it gives a broader outlook on life.'

The Way Ahead

The last few years have seen many changes in the Irish economy. Industry has grown, while unemployment has fallen, leading the media to nickname the booming economy 'the Celtic Tiger'. Economic growth is expected to slow down, and problems such as long-term unemployment, poverty and the need to reduce dependency on money from the EU have still to be tackled, but the Celtic Tiger is alive and kicking. Meanwhile, as immigration figures show, Ireland is becoming an increasingly popular place to live, with a reputation for being vibrant and friendly.

▲ *Dublin, Ireland's capital city, is a major tourist destination.*

The euro (€)

On 1 January 2002, Ireland became one of the first countries to introduce the euro. The currency changeover was smooth, it is now easier for European tourists to spend their money, and there is a real feeling of partnership with the rest of Europe.

▶ *The modern financial centre in Dublin is at the heart of Ireland's recent economic success.*

IN THEIR OWN WORDS

'My name is Mark Kelleher, and I've just started studying Economics at University College Dublin. Ireland has changed a great deal over the last twenty or thirty years. When my parents were young, the nearest cinema was 130 km away. Now it's only 25 km away. There are also more airports, shops and restaurants. The downside is that Ireland is now one of the most expensive places to live in Europe. I'm worried that prices will rise still further and whether the EU will continue to support our country. However, that's all in the future, so we'll just have to wait and see what happens!'

A changed country

In 1845, Ireland was a country that could not afford to feed its people. At the beginning of the twenty-first century, Ireland gives more to charity per person than any other Western European country. Irish donors give especially generously to charities helping those suffering from starvation. The country has stepped out of the shadow of Great Britain and has forged strong links with the USA and with Europe. Ireland is looking forward to an exciting and prosperous future.

▶ *Irish people give generously to charity.*

Glossary

Alternative medicine Types of medicine considered to be unorthodox by the medical profession.

Bituminous coal A type of soft, black coal that burns with a very bright, smoky flame.

Capacity The amount that something can contain.

Census An official survey of the population, carried out at regular intervals (e.g. every ten years).

Civil war A war between citizens of the same country.

Colony A country or area that is controlled by another country.

Constitution Principles by which a country or state is governed.

Currency fluctuations Changes in the value of a currency compared with other currencies.

Denomination A branch of a church or a religion.

Economy All the activity involved in producing, buying and selling goods, which determines how wealthy a country is.

EEC European Economic Community, a group of countries that worked together to improve trade between member countries and later became the European Union.

Emigration When people leave their own country and go to live in another country.

Entrepreneur A businessperson who is prepared to take risks and try new ideas in order to make money.

European Union (EU) A group of European countries that work together to achieve economic and social progress and strengthen Europe's role in the world.

Export A product that is sold to another country

Fossil fuels Fuels made from the remains of plants and animals that died millions of years ago, including coal, oil and natural gas.

GNP per capita GNP is gross national product, the total value of all the goods and services a country produces in a year, including investments in the country by other nations. 'Per capita' means 'per person', so GNP per capita is the total value of the goods produced, divided by the total population.

Greenhouse-gas emissions Gases such as carbon dioxide that are released into the air as waste products from industries and vehicles. These gases build up in the Earth's atmosphere and trap heat from the Sun, leading to an increase in temperatures around the world.

Gulf Stream A warm ocean current that flows from the Gulf of Mexico towards north-west Europe.

Herbicides Chemicals used to kill weeds.

Hydroelectric power Electricity generated from turbines that are turned by the force of falling water.

Immigration When people leave their own country and come to live in a new country.

Insecticides Chemicals used to kill insect pests that attack crops.

Irish Free State The country formed from twenty-six Irish counties in 1921 and under the rule of an Irish government. In 1949, it became known as the Republic of Ireland.

Life expectancy The average length of time a person can expect to live.

Meteorologist A person who studies the Earth's atmosphere in order to find out about and forecast the weather.

Negotiations Discussions that aim to reach an agreement or compromise between different groups.

Partition The division in 1921 of the country of Ireland into two parts – the Irish Free State (which later became the Republic of Ireland) and Northern Ireland.

Peninsula A long, thin strip of land that is surrounded on three sides by water.

Pharmaceutical companies Companies that produce medical drugs.

Phosphorous Containing phosphorus, a chemical used in pesticides and fertilizers.

Pilgrimage A journey made to show the strength of a person's faith in their religion.

Rebellion An attack designed to show opposition to a government or other authority.

Renewable energy Energy such as wind or wave power that can be used again and again, unlike coal, for example, which can only be burnt once.

Smog A mixture of smoke and fog.

Taoiseach The Irish Prime Minister

Trade When something is bought or sold.

Further Information

Sources

The Truth about the Irish
by Terry Eagleton (New Island, 2002)

Culture Shock! Ireland
by Patricia Levy (Kuperard, 2000)

The Course of Irish History
by T W Moody and F X Martin (Mercier, 2001)

Black Hole, Green Card – The disappearance of Ireland
by Fintan O'Toole (New Island Books, 1994)

Understanding Contemporary Ireland – State, Class and Development in the Republic of Ireland
by Richard Breen, Damian F Hannan, David B Rottman & Christopher T Whelan (Gill and Macmillan, 1990)

Further reading
Books to read

Country Files: Ireland (Watts Books, 2002)
Fiesta!: Ireland (Watts Books, 2001)
The Irish Famine by Tony Allen (Heinemann Library, 2001)

For older readers

McCarthy's Bar by Pete McCarthy (Sceptre Lir, 2000)
The Road to McCarthy by Pete McCarthy (Sceptre Lir, 2002)

Index

Numbers in bold are pages where there is a photograph or illustration.